SAVANNAH
The Cubby 2024
Long Weekend Guide

No business listed in this guide has provided *anything* free to the author.

James Cubby

Fisher Collins Press

SAVANNAH
The Cubby
Long Weekend Guide

TABLE OF CONTENTS

Chapter 1
WHY SAVANNAH?

Every time I visit Savannah, I ask myself the same question: what is it about this fair city that I like so much?

An impossible question (for me) to answer. The culture? The food (Ah, yes, the food!)? The people? The charming layout of the city?

It's all of those things, of course. Savannah is a much more interesting city than Charleston because you can basically see what there is to see in Charleston in a day. A Long Weekend is more than ample time to savor the riches of Charleston (excluding its numerous fine restaurants) unless you venture to some of the plantations outside town.

Not so Savannah. You'll need a lot more than a Long Weekend to take in everything Savannah has to offer, trust me.

Of all historic figures, Civil War General William Sherman is largely responsible for preserving the city by the simple act of *not* burning it down when he made his famous March to the Sea, destroying everything in his Army's path—except Savannah.

My first experience here was as an undergrad when I came to meet the parents of my college girlfriend. Theirs was one of the older families in Savannah, and their name even graces one of its most famous squares.

Speaking of those famous squares, the layout of Savannah makes it very interesting. There are 21 squares that give this city a strong human scale other U.S. cities will never have. Savannah feels more like London than any other American city to my mind (except of course for the weather). These squares, sometimes frustrating for motorists who have to navigate around them, make cycling around Savannah a pleasure.

There used to be 24 squares in the original plan of the city, but 3 of these were sacrificed to developers who demolished them before the people came to their senses and stopped the wanton destruction of Savannah's valuable heritage. Another square, Ellis, once no more than a parking lot, is now looking more like it did in the old days.

A little side note: famed lyricist Johnny Mercer, who wrote some 1,600 songs and took home 4 Oscars for Best Song, was from here. He was one of the great contributors to the Great American Songbook. (He wrote "Moon River," for example, which Audrey Hepburn sang not so well in "Breakfast at Tiffany's.")

Be certain to visit the **River Street Pedestrian District**. Here you'll see water taxis, riverboats, and numerous private craft plying the river. The waterfront is lined with shops, restaurants and quite a few tourist traps. Still, it's great to see it.

Chapter 2
GETTING ABOUT

<u>CAR</u>

Unless you're going to be staying downtown in the Historic District, you will need a car.

<u>PUBLIC TRANSIT</u>

CAT
Chatham Area Transit
<u>www.catchacat.org</u>
Bus service throughout Savannah. There's a free
CAT Shuttle (Route #1) that serves the Historic
District.

<u>STREETCAR</u>

<u>CONNECTONTHEDOT</u>
<u>www.connectonthedot.com</u>
The River Street Streetcar runs 1 mile along an old streetcar line in the Downtown Historic District. It has 12 stops on its route.

<u>FERRY</u>

There's a free **Savannah Belles Ferry** that runs across the Savannah River, linking the Historic District and Convention Center on Hutchinson Island.

<u>WALKING</u>

In the Historic District, you can do a lot of walking. Park your car and go out on foot.

Information:
<u>www.savannahvisit.com</u>

MLK Visitor Information Center
301 Martin Luther King, Jr. Blvd., Savannah, 912-944-0455
<u>www.visitsavannah.com/profile/mlk-visitor-information-center/6155</u>

Tybee Island Visitor Information Center
1st St, Tybee Island, 912-786-5444
<u>www.visittybee.com/travel-aid/tybee-visitor-center</u>

Visitor Center at Ellis Square
26 Barnard St, Savannah, 912-525-3100 x 1343

Savannah/ Hilton Head International Airport Visitor Center
400 Airways Ave, Savannah, 912-964-0514
www.savannahairport.com/at-the-airport/visitor-information-center

Visit Savannah Visitor Information Center
101 E Bay St, Savannah, 912-644-6400
www.visitsavannah.com

The River Street Visitor Information Center
1 W River St, Savannah, 912-651-6662
https://www.visitsavannah.com/profile/the-river-street-visitor-information-center/6159

Chapter 3
WHERE TO STAY

Savannah has an endless selection of bed-and-breakfasts, including several that are said to be haunted, that range between $200 and $300 a night. The **Association of Historic Inns of Savannah** has listings at www.historicinnsofsavannah.com

THE 17HUNDRED90 INN
307 E President St, Savannah, 912-236-7122
www.17hundred90.com
This historic inn has 14 comfortable rooms, each with king or queen sized bed, private bath, a growing

collection of antiques. A stop on most of Savannah's ghost tours and it's said there are ghosts still wandering the rooms.

BALLASTONE
14 E Oglethorpe Ave, Savannah, 912-236-1484
www.ballastone.com
Listed on the National Register of Historic Places, guests feel like they're stepping back to the Victorian era once they enter this beautiful inn that has been elegantly furnished with antiques and fine reproductions. The inn offers 13 guestrooms and 3 suites, all uniquely decorated, some with canopied beds and beamed ceilings. Many rooms have working gas fireplaces and three have whirlpool tubs. Amenities include: Free Wi-Fi, TVs, daily newspapers, morning breakfast, afternoon tea served on fine china, and an evening social hour with hors

d'oeuvres. The inn has its own private Victorian bar
fully stocked with boutique wines.

BOHEMIAN HOTEL
102 W Bay St, Savannah, 912-721-3800
www.bohemianhotelsavannah.com
Here the old meets the new as design elements
celebrate the 18th century era but with modern
luxuries. Amenities include: concierge services,
fitness center, 37-inch LCD TVs, and complimentary
wireless Internet access. Rooms feature Historic
District or Riverfront views. This is a pet-friendly and
smoke-free hotel. On-site restaurant and lounge
featuring live music.

THE BRICE
601 E Bay St, Savannah, 912-238-1200
www.bricehotel.com
The elegant Brice Hotel, shiny as a new penny,
features 145 guestrooms including 26 suites. Big
floor-to-ceiling windows look out over Washington
Square. The 1860s building has almost as storied a
history as Savannah itself. It's been a cotton
warehouse, Coca-Cola bottling plant, a stable, among
other things. It's a Kimpton property, so you can be
sure it's a fun and lively place to stay, with a
whimsical ambience and playful designs. Here you'll
be welcomed with Southern hospitality and enjoy the
lavish extras one would expect from a grand old
Savannah hotel. Amenities include outdoor pool
fringed with palm trees, free bikes, free coffee and tea
in the lobby every morning (and free wine daily at the
cocktail hour), in-room spa services available, free

Wi-Fi, flat-screen TVs with cable channels, and iPod docks. Smoke-free hotel. On-site bar/lounge, the **Pacci Italian Kitchen & Bar**, is a large open space, serving items like Cola glazed short ribs with mushroom risotto. Pet friendly hotel.

EAST BAY INN

225 E. Bay St., 800-500-1225
www.eastbayinn.com
The rooms here at this B&B tend to be a little larger than you see elsewhere. Some rooms have 4-posters, others have two large queen size beds, some are pet-friendly. Lots of great moldings and dark woods that really give you the feel you're in an old Victorian mansion. (The creaky floors do, too!) Free newspapers in the morning, bellman service, breakfast in the morning—they offer a lot of extras touches you'll appreciate.

FOLEY HOUSE INN

14 Hull St, Savannah, 800 647 3708
www.foleyinn.com
This authentic bed and breakfast inn offers a variety
of room options; all 19-guest rooms are uniquely
decorated to complement the time and historical
heritage. Amenities include: complimentary
breakfast, afternoon sweets and tea, evening wine and
hors d'oeuvres, complimentary morning paper and
comfy cotton bathrobes. This is a perfect setting for a
romantic getaway. Conveniently located near the
Historic District, shopping, and other local
attractions. All rooms are non-smoking.

THE GALLOWAY HOUSE B&B

107 E. 35th St, Savannah, 912-658-4419
www.thegallowayhouse.com
Located in the heart of the Historical District, this
charming three-level Bed & Breakfast offers private 1
or 2 bedroom apartments. Amenities include:
unlimited breakfast in your apartment whenever you

choose, complimentary secure Wi-Fi, and HDTV with DIRECTV. Pet friendly.

HOTEL TYBEE
1401 Strand Ave, Tybee Island, 912-786-7777
www.hoteltybee.com
If you'd rather be near the expansive beaches on Tybee Island than in the middle of the Historic District, this resort features 208 rooms and suites on the beach near Tybee Pier. Rooms are spacious and many have private balconies. Dine on-site at A-J's Beachside Restaurant and Bar specializing in fresh seafood with a Southern twist.

KEHOE HOUSE
123 Habersham St., 912-232-1020
www.kehoehouse.com
Built in 1893 for William Kehoe of Kehoe Ironworks. What looks like white wooden trim is actually iron. Located in the Historic District, this exquisitely restored 1892 mansion offers 13 guestrooms all decorated with elegant furnishings and antiques. Amenities include: Cooked-to-order breakfast, wine and hors d'oeuvres reception, homemade desserts & coffee service, 24-hour concierge, CD & DVD players, wireless internet, and turndown service. An Adults-Only B&B.

THE MARSHALL HOUSE
123 E Broughton St, Savannah, 912-644-7896
www.marshallhouse.com
Savannah's oldest hotel, built in 1851 and restored in
1999. The hotel has 68 rooms, some with antique
clawfoot tubs and access to a wrought-iron balcony.

MONTAGE AT PALMETTO BLUFF
477 Mount Pelia Rd, Bluffton, 855-264-8705
www.montagehotels.com/palmettobluff/
This inn (a bit out of town from Savannah) offers
charming cottages and village homes surrounding the
Inn on 20,000 acres of property overlooking the May
River. You stay in one of the cottages but the focal
point is the Inn itself where you can enjoy shrimp and
grits for breakfast. You zip around in golf carts.
Amenities offered include outdoor pool, lap pool, and
spa facility. Variety of outdoor activities available for
guests. On-site fine dining.

PLANTERS INN
29 Abercorn St, Savannah, 912-232-5678 or 800-554-1187
www.plantersinnsavannah.com
Located in downtown Savannah, this elegant hotel offers extravagant amenities and beautifully appointed rooms. Amenities include: free wine & cheese social, nightly turndown service, expanded continental breakfast delivered to your room, free USA Today newspapers, digital cable/satellite TV, free wireless internet access, and free bottled water. Conveniently located near the Historic District and attractions like the Telfair Museum of the Arts, Gordon Low House, River Street and City Market. Guests enjoy dining at The Olde Pink House, one of Savannah's most popular restaurants, located next door to the Planters Inn.

PRESIDENTS' QUARTERS INN
225 E President St, Savannah, 912-233-1600
www.presidentsquarters.com
This historic boutique hotel offers 16 richly appointed suites – some featuring balconies overlooking the courtyard, decorated in antique and period reproduction furniture. Amenities include: Free gourmet breakfast, afternoon hors d'oeuvres, cable TV, free Wi-Fi, and free on-site parking.

RIVER STREET INN

124 E. Bay St., Savannah, 912-234-6400
www.riverstreetinn.com

The River Street Inn, located at the beginning of
Savannah's Landmark district, is an intimate 86-room
guest hotel that overlooks the Savannah River. Guests
are treated to the charm of the past mixed with
modern conveniences and personal amenities. Guest
rooms feature private baths with brass bath fixtures,
exquisite furnishings and hardwood floors. Amenities
include: free morning newspaper, afternoon wine &
hors d'oeuvres reception, homemade chocolates as
you retire for the evening, free coffee, in-room
movies, data port & Wi-Fi. Conveniently located
near Savannah's Historic District, local attractions,

museums, antique shops, shopping, and restaurants. 100% non-smoking hotel. Four on-site restaurants, and variety of on-site shopping.

THE THUNDERBIRD INN
611 W Oglethorpe Ave, Savannah, 912-232-2661
www.thethunderbirdinn.com
A no-frills motel recently refurbished. Conveniently located near attractions like the Telfair Museum of Art, Thunderbird offers 42 air-condition guestrooms. Amenities include: free wireless Internet access, TVs with premium cable channels, free breakfast, and tour/ticket assistance. This is a smoke-free property. Southern hospitality perks include Moon Pies on guests' pillows and Krispy Kreme donuts delivered hot at dawn.

THE WESTIN SAVANNAH HARBOR GOLF RESORT & SPA

1 Resort Drive, Savannah, 912-201-2000
www.westinsavannah.com
This resort and spa is a mixture of modern luxury and Southern charm. Located directly across the river from the heart of the Historic District. To get over, they have a free 2-minute ferry ride that takes you to River Street. The great advantage of staying here, of course, is that you're close to the Historic District, but you have all the modern amenities you won't find in your typical B&B. They have an 18-hole PGA golf course, the **Heavenly Spa** and there's also a beautiful pool and beach club. There's a pool bar and grill, a lounge, and the **Aqua Star** features award-winning seafood cuisine from Chef Roger Michel.

Chapter 4
WHERE TO EAT

45 BISTRO
123 E Broughton St, Savannah, 912-234-3111
www.45bistro.com
CUISINE: American
DRINKS: Full Bar
SERVING: Dinner
PRICE RANGE: $$$
Located adjacent to the historic Marshall House, here you'll enjoy some of Savannah's finest dining. Chef Ryan Behneman prepares dishes like lasagna of

jumbo sea scallops, wilted spinach, mascarpone cheese and a tomato ragu and filet of salmon gratinéed with sautéed hearts of palm and artichokes.

A-J's DOCKSIDE RESTAURANT
1315 Chatham Ave, Tybee Island, 912-786-9533
www.ajsdocksidetybee.com
CUISINE: Seafood
DRINKS: Full Bar
SERVING: Dinner
PRICE RANGE: $$
Tucked into a quiet waterfront corner on the island's south side. Here you'll find some of the best seafood on the island. Try favorites like the shrimp and grits or artichoke dip appetizers, or a bowl of crab stew or scored flounder. Arrive early for dinner.

BACK IN THE DAY BAKERY

2403 Bull St, Savannah, 912-495-9292
www.backinthedaybakery.com
An old-fashioned bakery that's a favorite among
locals, tourists and foodies. Not just a bakery but also
a café with a delicious menu of sandwiches, like the
Madras curry chicken on ciabatta. Here you'll find
Savannah's best desserts, artisan breads, award
winning cupcakes along with great coffee and
espresso. Free Wi-Fi.

BOAR'S HEAD GRILL & TAVERN

1 N Lincoln St, Savannah, 912-651-9660
www.boarsheadgrillandtavern.com
CUISINE: American
DRINKS: Full Bar
SERVING: Lunch & Dinner
PRICE RANGE: $$

Located in the historic section of Savannah, Chef
Philip Branan prepares a delicious selection of steaks,
chops and seafood.

CLARY'S CAFÉ

404 Abercorn St, Savannah, 912-233-0402
www.claryscafe.com
Steeped in local history, Clary's, in business since
1903, serves breakfast all day including omelets,
grits, steaming biscuits and plain, pecan strawberry
and blueberry malted waffles. The restaurant is
covered with knickknacks, paintings, family pictures
and memorabilia.

COLLINS QUARTER

2 locations
151 Bull St, Savannah, 912-777-4147
621 Drayton St, Savannah, 912-298-6532
https://www.thecollinsquarter.com/
CUISINE: Breakfast/American (New) / Australian
DRINKS: Full Bar
SERVING: Breakfast, Lunch, & Dinner – No Dinner
on Mondays & Tuesdays
PRICE RANGE: $$
NEIGHBORHOOD: Historic District
Two coffee cafes serving brunch all day and creative
lunch and dinner options. It's more a spirited café
during the day, but at night they light candles to give
the place a more intimate, romantic aura. Favorites:
Aussie Based Avocado Smash; Short Rib Hash is a
standout; Ahi Tuna Poke. Innovative cocktails and
extensive wine list. Impressive coffee menu.
Reservations recommended.

COTTON & RYE

1801 Habersham St, Savannah, 912-777-6286
http://www.cottonandrye.com/
CUISINE: American (New)
DRINKS: Full Bar
SERVING: Dinner (Closed Sundays & Mondays)
PRICE RANGE: $$$
NEIGHBORHOOD: Thomas Square
Set in a former 1950s bank, this gastropub offers a creative menu of New American fare. There's a nice bar inside, but if the weather's nice, I always opt for a table on their outdoor deck. Favorites: Shrimp & Grits and Fried Chicken with Mac and Cheese. (There are many great versions of fried chicken in Savannah, but if this is your first trip, you could do worse than get it here—and since you're getting fried chicken, get their mac & cheese to go with it.) Amazing cocktails.

DECK BEACH BAR AND KITCHEN

404 Butler Ave., Tybee Island, 912-328-5397
www.thedecktybee.com
CUISINE: American (New)/Seafood
DRINKS: Full Bar
SERVING: Lunch & Dinner; Closed Mon – Wed.
PRICE RANGE: $$
Less than a half-hour from Savannah, this is the only
bar / restaurant on the sand in Tybee with ocean
views from every seat. Favorites: Vietnamese style
shrimp Po Boy sandwich and Chicken Satay
sandwich. The seafood platter here is big enough to
satisfy 2 or even 3. It's tempura cod made with a
beer-batter, grilled shrimp, fried calamari, snow crab
legs, ahi tuna poke (they say it's ahi tuna, but

probably not), corn on the cob, vinegar fries, sweet potato fries and a good portion of island-style cole slaw. (I was with one other person when we ordered it, and we brought home enough to feed another person.) The good thing about this seafood platter is that it's not all fried, like so many others. Vegetarian options. Dining inside or on the deck. Happy hour. The view makes this a great brunch spot. Go for a walk on the beach to work up an appetite. (Note the closed days above.)

ELIZABETH ON 37TH
105 E 37th St, Savannah, 912-236-5547
www.elizabethon37th.net
CUISINE: American
DRINKS: Full Bar
SERVING: Dinner
PRICE RANGE: $$$

Chef Kelly Yambor serves up fresh seafood in an elegant stately mansion dating back to the early 20th Century. Favorites include the shrimp and grits with red-eye gravy, traditionally made from leftover coffee, Bluffton oysters served three ways, including raw with tomato-cilantro; snapper with a chewy crust of shredded potato and asiago cheese; spicy red rice & shrimp; clams with roasted Vidalia onions. They use house grown herbs and edible flowers in their dishes. There's a 7-course tasting menu available that's a good bet. Excellent service from beginning to end.

EMPORIUM KITCHEN AND WINE MARKET
254 E Perry St., Savannah, 912-559-8400
www.emporiumsavannah.com
CUISINE: American (New)
DRINKS: Full Bar
SERVING: Breakfast, Lunch, & Dinner

PRICE RANGE: $$
Popular eatery offering locally sourced, quality menu items, but it's also part market, part coffee shop, a bistro-style feel to it and a take-away option. Favorites: Local Salmon en Papillote; Roasted BBQ oysters; and Rabbit Ragout with House-Made Pappardelle. Bar on first floor and rooftop, ice cream bar and wine area, and games on rooftop.

FLYING MONK NOODLE BAR

5 W Broughton St, Savannah, 912-232-8888
www.flywiththemonk.com
CUISINE: Vietnamese
DRINKS: Beer & Wine Only
SERVING: Lunch & Dinner
PRICE RANGE: $$
This popular eatery offers a menu restaurant featuring pan-Asian noodle dishes. Noodle dishes from a variety of Asian nations are represented including Vietnam, Malaysia, China, Thailand, Korea, and Laos. Menu favorites include: Pho beef and Peking Duck.

FOX & FIG

321 Habersham St, Savannah, 912-297-6759
https://foxandfigcafe.com/
CUISINE: Vegan/Breakfast
DRINKS: Wine & Beer
SERVING: Breakfast, Lunch, & Dinner
PRICE RANGE: $$
NEIGHBORHOOD: Troup Square
High-end vegan café featuring a variety of vegan
options, coffees, milkshakes, and lattes. (Non-dairy.)
I'm not big on vegan food as a rule, but my girlfriend
loves it, and she really loves this place. Favorites:

Chipotle Mac & Cheese and the Fox Burger. Outdoor seating. Dog friendly.

FOXY LOXY CAFÉ
1919 Bull St, Savannah, 912-401-0543
www.foxyloxycafe.com
CUISINE: Espresso Bar/Tex-Mex
DRINKS: Beer & Wine
SERVING: Breakfast, Lunch, Desserts
PRICE RANGE: $
A cute little place with a small menu but they serve excellent craft beers and delicious tacos. There's also a nice dessert selection, great coffees and they serve breakfast all day. Live music on Tuesday nights.

It's close & tight at Geneva's, but the food's spectacular.

GENEVA'S FAMOUS CHICKEN AND CORNBREAD CO.

1909 Victory Dr, Savannah, 912-235-2978
https://www.eatgenevas.com/
CUISINE: Southern
DRINKS: No Booze
SERVING: Lunch, & Dinner (Closed Mondays)
PRICE RANGE: $$
NEIGHBORHOOD: Olympus/Victory Square
Small down-home eatery (with only a few tables inside and a couple outside with a handful of chairs at the counter) offering authentic Southern fare focusing on chicken, seafood, and homemade vegetable dishes. This is the real thing, folks. Favorites: Fried Chicken and Mac & Cheese. Most places in the South have "their own" cornbread recipe, which is fine, but here they cleverly offer delicious cornbread in a variety of flavors, such as jalapeño and blueberry, which I really love.

GREEN TRUCK PUB
2430 Habersham St., 912-234-5885
www.greentruckpub.com
CUISINE: Pubs, Burgers
DRINKS: Beer & Wine
SERVING: Lunch, dinner, Tuesday-Saturday
PRICE RANGE: $$
The crew at the Green Truck Pub, just a parking lot away from the Habersham antiques mall, makes simple food from scratch, sourcing as many of their ingredients as they can locally. They use grass-fed beef from Hunter Cattle in nearly Brooklet, and their pork and free-range chicken are raised in Georgia. They buy their coffee beans from Perc Coffee just a few blocks away. Produce is selected at the farmer's market at nearby Forsyth Park. Popular menu items include the Rustico burger with goat cheese, balsamic caramelized onions, roasted red peppers and fresh basil that they grow in their backyard garden; the Whole Farm, a bacon-cheddar burger topped with a fried egg; the California BLT has avocado; one of my favorites here is the Grilled Cheese with bacon and tomato. Add the hand-cut fries and you're all set. They have a rotating selection of about 30 craft beers.

THE GREY
109 Martin Luther King Jr Blvd, Savannah, 912-662-5999
www.thegreyrestaurant.com
CUISINE: American (New) / Bistro
DRINKS: Full Bar
SERVING: Lunch & Dinner; closed Mon

PRICE RANGE: $$$

Located in a sleek refurbished 1938 Greyhound bus depot from the Art Deco era, this high-end eatery offers a pleasing menu of Southern fare from Chef Mashama Bailey. The kitchen was installed in what used to be the ticket booth. Fancy décor with steel-blue booths, terrazzo floors. There was a 24-hour diner in the old bus station that has been remodeled into an elegant bar. The chef was born in the Bronx, but has steeped herself in Southern cuisine. Try her spicy BBQ sauce she slathers on her chicken schnitzel sandwich. Nice wine list with a focus on European labels. This is a good place to begin a night on the town. Reservations highly recommended.

GRYPHON TEA ROOM
337 Bull St., Savannah, 912-525-5880
www.scadgryphon.com
CUISINE: Tea Room/American fare
DRINKS: No Booze
SERVING: Lunch & Dinner
PRICE RANGE: $
American café known for their sumptuous tea service
that's situated on the wonderful Madison Square in
the handsome Scottish Rite Masonic Temple that
dates back to 1926. Gryphon is part of the Savannah

College of Art & Design. Though they have a great short menu, including delectable sandwiches, the tea is what you'll want to come here for. Impressive selection of teas served with tea sandwiches, scones and Devonshire cream & jam. That said, I might add they have an excellent brunch menu as well, with a full English breakfast which includes a sweet potato hash that's out of this world. Favorites: Asian-marinated salmon and Maple-glazed pork loin. There's outdoor seating on the red-bricked sidewalk.

HUSK
12 W Oglethorpe Ave., Savannah, 912-349-2600
www.husksavannah.com
CUISINE: Southern/Desserts
DRINKS: Full Bar
SERVING: Lunch & Dinner

PRICE RANGE: $$

Set in a landmark mansion, this elegant eatery offers a menu of Southern fare, but with a unique twist shared by its other outposts in Charleston and Nashville (among other cities). They strive to use the "indigenous ingredients" of coastal Georgia. And they do it so well. As a rule, the first meal I eat when I get to Charleston is at Husk. Now the same is true in Savannah. Menu changes daily, depending on what's available that's fresh and in season. Favorites: Hot Fried Chicken with Bradford Collards; Glazed pork ribs with pickled Georgia peaches (those peaches are SO good); and Mark's Tilefish. Order a side of sour dough bread for the table – you won't be disappointed. Upstairs bar. Nice wine selection.

Interior of HUSK – just one of the rooms

THE LADY AND SONS
102 W Congress St, Savannah, 912-233-2600
www.ladyandsons.com
CUISINE: Southern
DRINKS: Full bar
SERVING: Lunch and dinner daily
PRICE RANGE: $$-$$$
This is the place that launched Paula Deen, the place
that inspired her first cookbook that led to stardom on
the Food Network. Always a busy place. The sons
mentioned are Jamie and Bobby. This 3-floor
complex serves some 8,000 or 9,000 people a week.
Three separate tour groups offer Paula Deen tours that
will take visitors to her restaurant and the one she
operates with her brother on Tybee Island as well as
some other Deen-related stops. The menu is
extensive, one of those "something for everything"
kind of menus you see at a national chain. And I don't
particularly like the place because you feel like one of
the cattle that end up in the burgers when you come

here. This is not to say the food is less than good: crab cakes, crab stuffed Portobello, fried green tomatoes, black pepper shrimp, fried okra, crab stew cup. There's even an all you can eat Southern Buffet. I do, however, stop in often to buy things from their store. (People love things I get here as gifts.)

LOCAL 11 TEN FOOD & WINE
1110 Bull St, Savannah, 912-790-9000
www.local11ten.com
CUISINE: New Southern
DRINKS: Full bar (excellent wine list)
SERVING: Dinner nightly from 6
PRICE RANGE: $$
Though the building is in an unassuming structure that used to be a bank a block from Forsyth Park, inside you'll find an elegant room with sky-high ceilings, blond paneled walls. The people here insist on listing the farms where the vegetables came from, the company that delivered fish caught that day, the cheese monger who produced their cheeses, the guy who cured their bacon, the company that made their grits. Maybe they push this element too hard, but the results speak for themselves.

They *care* about their food. Try the Caesar's salad here: made with local romaine lettuce, pecorino Romano, olives, bacon bits and their own croutons. You've never had a Caesar's salad like this. The charcuterie board features meats they cured themselves and even their own pickles. Main courses might include frog legs from North Carolina or Beaufort County octopus with shaved onion and marinated feta, or, one night I was there, I had the milk-braised lamb's belly. Boy, was it tender. Menu changes frequently. Bright idea: do the chef's tasting menu and enjoy the tour. (Wine list here is very good, by the way, one of the best in town.)

MADAME BUTTERFLY

110 W Congress St, Savannah, 912-999-8539
https://www.madamebutterflysavannah.com/
CUISINE: Korean Steakhouse
DRINKS: Full bar
SERVING: Dinner, Lunch on Sat. & Sun.
PRICE RANGE: $$
NEIGHBORHOOD: Historic District
A sleek steakhouse with a clean modern design, this
eatery features a variety of Korean style choices

including duck, Yakatori skewers, Korean BBQ (one of my favorites) and Wagu fillet. Some outdoor seating as well. Signature cocktails.

MASADA CAFÉ
2301 W Bay St, Savannah, 912-236-9499
No Website
CUISINE: Southern
DRINKS: No Booze
SERVING: Lunch
PRICE RANGE: $
Located in the United House of Prayer for All People, so you know the food is prepared with love. Here

you'll find no frills Southern cooking and it's all about good home cooked soul food. Order from a simple menu that includes crispy fried chicken, delicious mac 'n cheese, and sweet potatoes served with cinnamon and nutmeg. For the entire experience visit the 11 a.m. Sunday service then stay for lunch.

MRS. WILKES' DINING ROOM

107 W Jones St, Savannah, 912-232-5997
www.mrswilkes.com
CUISINE: Southern / Soul Food
DRINKS: No Booze
SERVING: Lunch – weekdays; closed Sat & Sun
PRICE RANGE: $$
This busy Southern diner offers a family experience
as lunch guests dine at communal tables. Tables are
covered with dishes like Fried chicken, sweet potato
soufflé, black-eyed peas, okra gumbo, corn muffins
and biscuits. Menu changes daily.

OLDE PINK HOUSE

23 Abercorn St, Savannah, 912-232-4286
www.plantersinnsavannah.com/the-olde-pink-house/
CUISINE: Southern
DRINKS: Full Bar

SERVING: Lunch, Dinner
PRICE RANGE: $$$
If you love Southern cooking then you must eat here, as the food is to die for. Menu favorites include: Fried Green Tomatoes and the Shrimp & Grits. The setting is lovely and each part of the house has a historical theme. Save room for dessert and have the Chocolate Mouse Bomb.

PACCI ITALIAN KITCHEN + BAR @ THE BRICE HOTEL
601 E Bay St, Savannah, 912-233-6002
www.paccisavannah.com
CUISINE: Italian
DRINKS: Full Bar
SERVING: Breakfast, Lunch & Dinner
PRICE RANGE: $$
This rustic restaurant/bar offers Chef Roberto Leoci's menu of locally sourced Italian cuisine. Menu favorites include: Prosciutto and Melon and Cubano Italiano – a delicious pasta dish.

RANCHO ALEGRE CUBAN

402 Martin Luther King Jr Blvd, Savannah, 912-292-1656

www.ranchoalegrecuban.com

CUISINE: Cuban/Seafood
DRINKS: Full Bar
SERVING: Lunch & Dinner
PRICE RANGE: $$

No frills but pleasant enough Cuban eatery serving traditional plates of Cuban, Caribbean, Spanish and Latin American fare. (So much for focus.) Favorites: Marinated steak and Paella (if you want Paella put in your order right away as it takes 40 minutes—the Paella here is prepared Valenciana style—quite delicious and bursting with flavors). Creative cocktails. The "Suicide" cocktail is deadly, LOL.

Latin Jazz on the weekends. Wines from the Argentine, since Cuba is mostly known for beer, daiquiris, mojitos, 1950s cars with new engines and lots and lots of potholes. Oh, and outdated Communism.

REPEAL 33
125 Martin Luther King Jr Blvd, Savannah, 912-200-9255
https://www.repeal33savannah.com/
CUISINE: American (New)
DRINKS: Full Bar

SERVING: Dinner, Sunday Brunch
PRICE RANGE: $$
NEIGHBORHOOD: Yamacraw Village
Hip speakeasy-style bar offering a menu of New American fare. Has a long bar that extends down the whole room, and a few bare-bones wooden tables and chairs scattered about. Favorites: City Ham wrapped asparagus Tempura and House-Made Charcuterie. Live music. Reservations recommended.

SANDFLY BBQ
8413 Ferguson Ave, Savannah, 912-356-5463
www.sandflybbq.com
CUISINE: Barbeque
DRINKS: Beer & Wine Only
SERVING: Lunch & Dinner; closed Sun
PRICE RANGE: $$
A popular eatery serving Savannah style BBQ. Here you can sample delicious BBQ sandwiches, combination plates and smoked meats – glorious Southern fare. Excellent ribs and baked beans. The

menu also includes a variety of specials of Southwestern, Cajun, and Creole cuisine.

Low Country Boil

SAVANNAH SEAFOOD SHACK

116 E Broughton St, Savannah, 912-344-4393
https://savannahseafoodshack.com/
CUISINE: Seafood
DRINKS: Wine & Beer
SERVING: Lunch, & Dinner
PRICE RANGE: $$
NEIGHBORHOOD: Historic District
Popular fast-casual eatery specializing in Southern-style seafood dishes. Favorites: Spicy Garlic Blue Crabs; Low Country Boils; Po-boys; and Fried Fish Tacos. Corn on the cob and Hush puppies are standout sides.

SENTIENT BEAN

13 E Park Ave, Savannah, 912-232-4447
www.sentientbean.com
CUISINE: Vegetarian
DRINKS: No Booze
SERVING: Breakfast, Lunch & Dinner (7 a.m. to 10 p.m.)
PRICE RANGE: $
This coffee shop is a treat to visit and the menu if filled with organic, homemade food. This is a vegetarian/vegan's delight serving fresh, local organic foods. Menu consists of salads, tortillas, sandwiches and homemade soups. Breakfast served all day. There's also live music, film, and open mic nights. Check out the website for the rotating schedule.

SIX PENCE PUB

245 Bull St, Savannah, 912-233-3151
www.sixpencepub.com
CUISINE: American Traditional
DRINKS: Full Bar

SERVING: Lunch & Dinner
PRICE RANGE: $$
Those favoring British-style pubs will feel at home here. The pub eats are strictly English fare and the beer selection is quite impressive.

SOHO SOUTH CAFÉ

12 W Liberty St, Savannah, 912-233-1633
www.sohosouthcafe.com
CUISINE: American
DRINKS: Beer & Wine Only
SERVING: Lunch
PRICE RANGE: $$
This funky café, located in a former auto repair garage, is operated by local artists. Menu includes dishes like eggs Savannah, an English muffin topped with a jumbo crab cake, poached egg, asparagus and béarnaise. Their slogan, and it's appropriate, is "Where Food is Art.""

SUNDAE CAFÉ

304 First St., Tybee Island, 912-786-7694
www.sundaecafe.com
CUISINE: Reinvented Southern
DRINKS: Full bar

SERVING: Lunch, Dinner
PRICE RANGE: $$
Fried green tomatoes are in lots of dishes of this
family-owned Tybee Island restaurant: you can get
them as an appetizer or on top of salad, a BLT or
even a burger. Other favorites: seafood cheesecake,
shrimp and grits and a variety of other seafood. Paula
Deen is said to like the double-cut pork chop.
Speaking of Deen, she's added their recipes for
Succotash, Apple Chutney and Buttermilk Biscuit
Blue Cheese Bread Pudding in her "Cooking with
Paula Deen" magazine.

TREYLOR PARK
115 E Bay St, Savannah, 888-873-9567
https://www.treylorpark.com/
CUISINE: American (New)
DRINKS: Full Bar
SERVING: Lunch, & Dinner
PRICE RANGE: $$
NEIGHBORHOOD: Historic District – North
Quick in-and-out kind of place serving Southern
'comfort food' grub with a few twists, not all of them

so great. Favorites: Cheese Steak Egg Rolls; Sloppy Joe and Pot Pie. Get the Bourbon Pecan Pie for dessert. Cocktail bar and some outdoor seating.

VIC'S ON THE RIVER
26 East Bay St, Savannah, 912-721-1000
https://www.vicsontheriver.com/
CUISINE: Southern/Seafood
DRINKS: Full Bar
SERVING: Lunch, & Dinner

PRICE RANGE: $$
NEIGHBORHOOD: Downtown
Overlooking the River, this place is set in disused cotton warehouse built in 1859, now repurposed as a fine-dining eatery specializes in classic Southern fare and seafood. They have several rooms with high ceilings overlooking the water. Expansive windows at street level offer a lovely view of the trees outside. Favorites: She Crab Soup; Braised Beef Short Rib served with sour cream mash; and Wreckfish. Creative cocktails like the Peach Martini. Save room for the wonderful Praline Cheesecake, which is worth the trip by itself. The Wine Bar and Piano Bar add to the ambiance. Reservations recommended.

VINNIE VAN GO-GO'S
317 W Bryan St, Savannah, 912-233-6394
www.vinnievangogo.com
CUISINE: Pizza
DRINKS: Beer & Wine Only
SERVING: Lunch & Dinner
PRICE RANGE: $
This popular indoor-outdoor pizza joint offers hearty crust pizza.

WALL'S BARBECUE

515 E York Ln, Savannah, 912-232-9754
No Website
CUISINE: Barbeque, Soul Food
DRINKS: No Booze
SERVING: Lunch & Dinner; has erratic operating
hours, but usually open weekends
PRICE RANGE: $
An out-of-the-way eatery is prized by locals. They
only have 3 tables or so but the food is just fine.
Thick crab cakes, plates of crab, chicken, fish or pork
served with sides of rice, coleslaw, collard greens or
okra. The deviled crab is good, and the ribs are
excellent, too.

WYLD DOCK BAR

2740 Livingston Ave, Savannah, 912-692-1219
http://www.thewylddockbar.com/
CUISINE: Seafood
DRINKS: Full Bar
SERVING: Lunch & Dinner; Closed Mondays
PRICE RANGE: $$
Waterside eatery serving New American fare about
15 or 20 minutes from Savannah where you'll get an
expansive view of marshlands. Fresh seafood daily.
Menu changes often, usually every month. Try the
Fresh catch and Fish tacos served in banana leaves;
Quail & Rabbit Sausage; Shrimp roll. Outdoor dining
with waterfront views of the desolate marshlands.
Locals' hangout.

ZUNZI'S

236 Drayton St, Savannah, 912-443-9555
www.zunzis.com
CUISINE: International/Sandwiches
DRINKS: No Booze
SERVING: Lunch
PRICE RANGE: $
Closed Sunday
This café offers a mixture of international cuisine (Swiss, Italian, South African, and Dutch). Menu favorites include: The Godfather (an amazing sandwich made of smoked sausage, chicken, cheese, lettuce and tomato) and the Portabella Sandwich. Ideal for a casual lunch on a nice day.

Chapter 5
NIGHTLIFE

ALLEY CAT LOUNGE
207 W Broughton St, Savannah, 912-677-0548
https://www.alleycatsavannah.com/
Hip dimly-lit basement bar stocking more than 500
spirits with one of the most impressive cocktail
menus in Savannah. Entrance through a door in the
back alley, down the stairs to the basement. You'll
feel like you're in a speakeasy. Classic cocktails.

AMERICAN LEGION SAVANNAH POST NO 135

1108 Bull St, Savannah, 912-233-9277

www.alpost135.com

A historic structure that was built in 1913, now houses the town's neighborhood bar. No frills bar with cheap drinks.

BETTER THAN SEX

410 W Broughton St, Savannah, 912-306-0309

https://www.betterthansexdesserts.com/location/better-than-sex-savannah/

Intimate dessert restaurant with a speakeasy-style atmosphere. Bar menu features unique items like chocolate and caramel covered wines. Perfect for a date night.

CLUB ONE

1 Jefferson St, Savannah, 912-232-0200
www.clubone-online.com
The site of The Lady Chablis Show until her passing
in September 2016. The club still offers cabaret with
a variety of performers. Cash only.

CRYSTAL BEER PARLOR

301 W Jones St, Savannah, 912-349-1000
www.crystalbeerparlor.com
This is Savannah's second oldest restaurant and a
favorite gathering spot for locals. Simple menu but

everything is fresh and prepared to order. Friendly servers and great selection of beers.

ELECTRIC MOON SKYTOP LOUNGE & MOON DECK

500 W River St, Savannah, 912-373-9070
https://www.plantriverside.com/venues/electric-moon-skytop-lounge/
Located on the roof of the JW Marriot Hotel, this rooftop lounge offers stunning river views, signature cocktails, and live music. Bar games and dancing.

LOST SQUARE

412 Williamson St, Savannah, 912-715-7000
https://www.thelostsquare.com/
Inviting rooftop bar offers beautiful panoramic views. Handcrafted cocktails and small bites. Outdoor seating.

PEACOCK LOUNGE
37 Whitaker St, Savannah, 912-239-6697
https://flocktothewok.com/peacock-lounge
Exclusive classic cocktail lounge located in the
basement level of Flock to the Wok with an alley
entrance. Curated cocktails and small bites.
Bartenders are real pros.

PLANTERS TAVERN

23 Abercorn St, Savannah, 912-232-4286
www.plantersinnsavannah.com/oldc-pink-house-
restaurant

A dimly lit, low-ceilinged bar in the basement of the
high-dollar Olde Pink House, a dignified restaurant in
a 1771 house. There's dining room upstairs but
downstairs is where all the action is. If you get a seat
by the fireplace you might decide to stay all night and
enjoy the live music.

ROCKS ON THE ROOF

102 West Bay St, Savannah, 912-721-3900
https://www.kesslercollection.com/bohemian-savannah/dining/
Located on the rooftop of the Bohemian Hotel Savannah Riverfront, this nice outdoor eatery offers special cocktails, small plates, and incredible views. Live music. Closes at midnight.

SAVANNAII SMILES DUELING PIANOS

314 Williamson St, Savannah, 912-527-6453
https://www.savannahsmilesduelingpianos.com/
High energy piano bar where the show is all-requests
playing everything from rock n roll, country, rap, to
current tunes. Stop in for dinner and a show or just
cocktails. A cash tip will get your request played.
Open until 2 a.m.

WET WILLIE'S

101 E River St, Savannah, 912-235-5651
https://www.wetwillies.com/Locations/Savannah-
GA-River-Street
Dinner and cocktails or just cocktails to go. Wet
Willie's has locations around the globe and are

known for serving the World's Greatest Daiquiris frozen drinks (but not for me—they give me head freeze that ruins my day). Bar menu includes lowest common denominator food items like chicken tenders (chewier than tender) and gumbo that competes with the gravy at KFC for best wallpaper paste. Cocktails available to go for strolling the waterfront, which helps add to the tackiness of that area.

Chapter 6
WHAT TO SEE & DO

ANDREW LOW HOUSE
329 Abercorn St, Savannah, 912-233-1828
www.andrewlowhouse.com
The Andrew Low House, overlooking Lafayette
Square, is an Italianate-style stucco building that
gives visitors a little insight into life in Savannah
more than 150 years ago. Andrew Low's daughter-in-
law, Juliette Gordon Low, founded the Girl Scouts of
the USA in the parlor and died in the house in 1927
making the house a popular destination for Girl Scout

troops. Visitors can tour the restored house that features 13-foot ceilings, period antiques, crystal chandeliers, Egyptian marble fireplaces and giant mahogany doors.

BATTLEFIELD PARK HERITAGE CENTER
300 Martin Luther King Blvd, Savannah, 912-651-6825
https://www.savannah.com/battlefield-park/
This Park is a memorial to the soldiers who fought and died for freedom. Battlefield Park commemorates the second bloodiest battle of the Revolutionary War on October 9, 1779. The **Roundhouse Railroad Museum** (now called the Georgia State Railroad Museum) is also located here with one of the nation's best surviving examples of pre-Civil War railroad structures.

BLUE ORB TOURS
22 W Bryan St, Savannah, 912-665-4258
www.blueorbtours.com
Founded in 2010, this tour is a great way to see haunted Savannah. They offer four different tours: Grave Tales Ghost Tour, Beyond Good and Evil Tour, Adults Only Dead of Night Ghost Tour and

Ghost City Haunted Pub Crawl. Tours are fun and more entertaining than scary but the guides are great storytellers. Times and rates vary depending on the tour.

BULL RIVER MARINA
8005 E US Hwy 80, Savannah, 912-897-7300
https://bullrivermarina.com
This small marina offers boat charters, fishing, rafting, and kayaking. Just a simple old building with

old boats and cool guys running the place. Rent a boat (with a captain) and go out to view the sunset.

FLANNERY O'CONNOR'S CHILDHOOD HOME

207 East Charlton St, Savannah, 912-233-6014
www.flanneryoconnorhome.org
This museum is housed in the former childhood home of acclaimed novelist and short story writer Flannery O'Conner. This house is restored to the Depression-era and guided tours of the home are available. Guests can view rare books in the Bruckeimer Library. The gift shop offers unique books and gifts. Free events are offered during the year including the Sunday lecture series. Open Fri through Wednesday. Closed Thursdays. Nominal admission fee.

FORSYTH PARK

Drayton Street, Savannah, 912-651-6610,
www.savannah.com/parks-savannah
Forsyth Park is a beautiful 30-acre city park located in Savannah's Historic District. Filled with magnificent oak and magnolia trees, the park features include walking paths, a café, a huge 19th-century fountain of trumpeting mermen and spouting swans, a Confederate Memorial Statue, two well-equipped playgrounds, and vast lawns often used for soccer and Frisbee. The park is also the site of free concerts.

FORT PULASKI NATIONAL MONUMENT

US Hwy 80 E, Savannah, 912-786-8182
Fort Pulaski, located between Savannah and Tybee Island, is an enormous Civil War-era fort that once

guarded Savannah. The Fort, a fine example of historic military architecture, acts as a large-scale outdoor exhibit featuring demilune, drawbridges, ditches, and dikes. An inside exhibit shows the history of Fort Pulaski. Visitors can participate in a variety of outdoor activities including hiking, biking, fishing, and bird watching.

GEORGIA STATE RAILROAD MUSEUM
655 Louisville Rd, Savannah, 912-651-6823
www.chsgeorgia.org/GSRM
A National Historic Landmark, the Roundhouse Railroad Museum is the oldest and largest existing nineteenth-century operations complex in the U.S. On display are passenger cars, steam and diesel locomotives, steam-powered machinery, model railroads, and a 126-foot brick smokestack. Thirteen of the original structures remain.

HEARSE TOURS

412 E Duffy St, Savannah, 912-695-1578
www.hearseghosttours.com
There's no better way to experience a Ghost Tour
than riding in a hearse. An open-top hearse can pick
you up at your hotel for this special Hearse Ghost
Tour. On this tour you'll see some of Savannah's
beautiful mansions and drive through the Historic
District. You'll also hear about some of Savannah's
most notorious murders, suicides, and deathbed tales.
Ghost tours are very popular in Savannah, named
America's Most Haunted City. Tours available every
day of the year.

JEPSON CENTER FOR THE ARTS

207 W York St, Savannah, 912-790-8800
www.telfair.org/visit/jepson
The Jepson Center features over 7,500 square feet of
gallery space, a 220-seat auditorium, and community
center, education studios, and ArtZeum-a unique,

3,500-square foot interactive gallery for children and families. The Jepson Center is home to the Telfair's **Kirk Varnedoe Collection** featuring works by artists such as Jasper Johns, Chuck Close, Roy Lichtenstein, Jeff Koons, Frank Stella, and Richard Avedon.

The **Telfair Museum of Art**, the oldest art museum in the South, wanted to expand, and the result is a light-filled building that won praise for its architect, Moshe Safdie. When they built the Jepson Center for the Arts, the planners preserved Savannah's cherished street grid by dividing the structure into two, and joining it with two glass bridges, while giving the museum much-needed space. The original 19th-century museum (121 Barnard Street) is home to the **Bird Girl**, the now-famous statue that adorns the cover of "Midnight in the Garden"; it was moved from Bonaventure Cemetery for her protection. The museum also operates tours of the nearly 200-year-old **Owens-Thomas House** (124 Abercorn Street). Nominal admission fee.

JULIETTE GORDON LOW BIRTHPLACE

10 E Oglethorpe Ave, Savannah, 912-233-4501
www.juliettegordonlowbirthplace.org
The birthplace of Juliette Gordon Low, the founder of
the Girl Scouts of the USA, is a beautiful house built
in 1821. This architectural gem has become a
destination for Girl Scout troupes.

MERCER WILLIAMS HOUSE

429 Bull St, Monterey Square, Savannah, 912-238-
0208
www.mercerhouse.com
This historic house, located on Monterey Square, was
built in the 1860s for the great grandfather of
songwriter Johnny Mercer. This architectural gem
was restored by Jim Williams, the antiques dealer
made famous in the now-classic book, *Midnight in
the Garden of Good and Evil*. Mr. Williams survived
three murder trials but he was indeed acquitted. Tour

guides tend to embellish the good part of the story as Mr. Williams' sister, Dorothy Kingery, still lives on the second floor where guests are not allowed. The guide will share descriptive details about the rest of the house, the formal courtyard, the nap-ready veranda, the Continental rococo and the Edwardian Murano glass.

OATLAND ISLAND WILDLIFE CENTER
711 Sandtown Rd, Savannah, 912-395-1212
www.oatlandisland.org
Just five miles east of Savannah, this environmental education center holds such wildlife as endangered Florida panthers, eastern timber wolves and a variety of birds of prey. You can wander the nature trail which winds through Low Country forest and marsh. Programs for children are available.

OLD SAVANNAH TOURS

250 MLK Jr Blvd., Savannah, 912-234-8128
www.oldsavannahtours.com
Ghost Tours are a favorite in Savannah and Old
Savannah Tours offers a 90-minute Ghostly Nights
tour starting at 7 p.m. aboard an open-air trolley.
Daytime trolley tours are also available through town.
Riders are given a map and can climb on or off
throughout the Historic District.

OLD TOWN TROLLEY TOURS

855-245-8992
www.trolleytours.com
Highlights the top Savannah attractions with 15 stops
and more than 100 points of interest.

OLD SAVANNAH TOURS

912-234-8128

https://oldsavannahtours.com

Old Savannah Tours are the longest-running trolleys in Savannah. Check out the website for the variety of tours.

SHANNON SCOTT TOURS

330 Bonaventure Rd, Savannah, 912-319-5600
www.shannonscott.com
One of Savannah's most popular tours is that of the
Bonaventure Cemetery and Shannon Scott's Journeys
are more than a tour. Scott is a storyteller and has
pioneered some of the city's first specialty tours and
this one is one of the best. While he offers tours of the
cemetery during the day, Savannah's number one tour
is Bonaventure Afterhours where you are literally
locked in the cemetery for 2 hours.

T. S. CHU'S

7726 Johnny Mercer Blvd, Savannah, 912-897-7795
No Website
Chu's convenience stores are located throughout
Savannah and Tybee Island. Not your typical
convenience mart, here you'll find everything from
car washes to beach rafts, sunscreen, fishing tackle
and hardware.

TYBEE ISLAND LIGHTHOUSE & MUSEUM

30 Meddin Dr, Tybee Island, 912-786-5801
www.tybeelighthouse.org
A tour of the Tybee Island Lighthouse features a 178-
step climb to the top but the breathtaking view is
worth the effort. **The Tybee Island Museum** is
located in Battery Garland. Choose a guided sunset
tour and you'll see one of the most beautiful coastal
sunsets in the world.

Chapter 7
SHOPPING & SERVICES

24 E STYLE DESIGN CO.
24 E Broughton St, Savannah, 912-446-1601
https://24estyle.com/
Owners Ruel and Delaine Joyner offer a unique design shop set in a 1921 department store building, where customers can find handmade furniture from Indonesia and Hungary that can be ordered with custom upholstery designed by the owners.

A.T. HUN GALLERY
302 W Saint Julian St, Savannah, 912-233-2060
www.athun.com
A staple in City Market for over 16 years, this gallery offers a colorful and eclectic group of art from 25 local and international artists. Much of the art found here is untraditional and unique.

ARCANUM ANTIQUES AND INTERIORS
14 W Jones St, Savannah, 912-236-6000
No Website
This antique and interior shop offers a variety of furniture and design pieces. You'll find original art, antiques, and contemporary furniture. Design services available.

BACK IN THE DAY BAKERY
2403 Bull St, Savannah, 912-495-9292
www.backinthedaybakery.com
This relaxed bakery lives by their motto, "Slow Down and Taste the Sweet Life." The bakery offers handcrafted baked goods like cakes, brownies, artisan breads, pies, cookies, and cupcakes as well as lunch fare and excellent coffee.

BLICK ART MATERIALS
318 E. Broughton St, Savannah, 912-234-0456
http://www.dickblick.com/stores/georgia/savannahbroughtonst/
This two-story art supply store is popular among SCAD students and local artists. The first floor features art supplies from spray paint to oil paints as well as office supplies and unique toys. Upstairs you

find drawing paper, canvases, glue, portfolios, and a variety of bags and totes.

THE BOOK LADY
6 E Liberty St, Savannah, 912-233-3628
www.thebookladybookstore.com
Located in the center of the Historic District, this shop offers over 50,000 new and used books in over 40 genres. The shop also offers event like book readings and signings, free Wi-Fi, and book clubs.

BRIGHTER DAY NATURAL FOODS
1102 Bull St, Savannah, 912-236-4703
www.brighterdayfoods.com
This natural food store is the ideal shop for vegetarians and vegans offering great products, fresh organic produce, vitamins and supplements, a deli and juice bar, and an outdoor café.

CHOCOLAT BY ADAM TURONI
323 W Broughton St, Savannah, 912-335-2914
www.chocolatat.com
Adam Turoni, Savannah's very own Chocolatier, offers up some of the best chocolates available. The décor is a chocolate lovers fantasy and the floor is faux grass. A variety of chocolate choices are available from the typical to the unusual including peanut butter cups, red velvet, pumpkin truffles, habanero truffles, Mayan chocolate truffles and

Bailey's Irish cream truffles. This is a self-serve shop
where you grab a tray and using a tong, select your
favorite chocolates.

COPPER PENNY

22 W Broughton St, Savannah, 912-629-6800
www.shopcopperpenny.com
This boutique offers upscale women's fashions and
footwear. Copper Penny collections feature a
Southern sensibility and style. Here you'll find
designer fashions, footwear, accessories and jewelry.

CUSTARD BOUTIQUE

422 Whitaker St, Savannah, 912-232-4733
www.custardboutique.com
This popular boutique carries a variety of fashions for
women including everything from shoes and

accessories to bags, designer dresses and gifts. Name brands offered include: French Connection, Super Maggie, By Boe, Tano, Gillian Julius, Jeffrey Campbell, ALL Black, and Miss Oops.

DAVIS PRODUCE

7755 U.S. Highway 80 E., 843-304-4989
https://www.facebook.com/pages/Davis-Produce/137652852924664?sk=info&tab=overview
If you're on your way to Tybee Island and want some fresh fruit to take to the beach, stop here. Or just grab a bag of boiled peanuts or a jar of salsa or pickles to take home. You can't miss this produce stand on Talahi Island, at Quarterman Drive and Highway 80 East.

E. SHAVER BOOKSELLER

326 Bull St, Savannah, GA 31401, (912) 234-7257
www.eshaverbooks.com
Located on Madison Square, this is Savannah's oldest bookstore. Here you'll find twelve rooms filled with fiction and non-fiction books. The shop specializes in

local and regional topics such as history, architecture, decorating, arts, and cooking. There's also a section dedicated to the Civil War.

FOLKLORICO
440 Bull St, Savannah, 912-232-9300
No Website
This beautiful, unique shop offers a selection of gift items not found in chain stores. What you'll find here is a nice selection of international "folk" art from more than 30 different countries. The shop also carries artifacts, iconography, accent furniture, ceramics, pottery, blown glass, textiles and contemporary art.

FORSYTH PARK FARMERS MARKET
South End of Forsyth Park, Savannah
www.forsythfarmersmarket.com
Open daily from 9 a.m. to 1 p.m. (rain or shine), this farmer's market offers a variety of vendors selling produce, hand-made products, local goods including eggs, honey, pastured meat, bread, cheese, mushrooms, herbs, preserves, coffee beans and plants.

FRESH MARKET
5525 Abercorn St #60, Savannah, 912-354-6075
www.thefreshmarket.com
Fresh Market is known for offering the freshest quality products, both locally and internationally. The market has an old world charm and visitors shop while listening to classical music. Here you'll find high-quality meats, fresh seafood, and local, organic produce.

GALLERY 209
209 E River St, Savannah, 912-236-4583
www.gallery209savannah.com
Two floors of original art, woodworking, crafts,
photography, jewelry, and gifts.

GLOBE SHOE CO.
17 E Broughton St., 912-232-8161
In the middle of one of the main streets in the touristy
Historic District, this shoe store is loaded with flats,
wedges and pumps by the high-quality shoemaker
Stuart Weitzman. You'll also find cute shoes by Via
Spiga, Ugg, Vaneli, Sam Edelman and Gentle Souls.
Paula Deen shops here (well, she used to—now, her
assistants pick up shoes for her to try on—she's
besieged with autograph seekers when she goes out).

GO FISH
106 W Broughton St, Savannah, 912-234-1260
www.shopgofish.com
This unique bohemian boutique features fashions,
shoes and accessories including lots of hand-made,
one-of-a-kind items from around the world. Here
you'll find hippie style dresses and many items
designed in-house by the owners.

GRAVEFACE RECORDS & CURIOSITIES
5 W 40th St, Savannah, 912-335-8018
www.facebook.com/mcpsociety
A unique shop that sells new and used vinyl records,
bitters, cocktail supplies, toys, games, taxidermy
(how about a rabbit bust or a rat's skull or sick-

looking dolls with fake blood dripping off them?), and performance equipment. Consignments available. This shop might even buy your old record collection. On-site video games – free play.

HALF MOON OUTFITTERS
15 E Broughton St, Savannah, 912-201-9393
www.halfmoonoutfitters.com
Since 1993, this shop has provided quality goods and services for adventure and travel. Here you'll find gear for paddle boarding, rock climbing, back packing, kayaking, trail running and other outdoor adventures. Look for name brands like The North Face, Patagonia, Mountain Hardwear, Smartwool and Keen.

HARLEY-DAVIDSON
1 Fort Argyle Rd, Savannah, 912-925-0005
503 E River St, Savannah, 912-231-8000
www.savannahhd.com
Here you'll find everything Harley-Davidson from motorcycles (new and pre-owned) to fashions, and accessories. Rentals, service, and even instructions available – home of Rider's Edge Academy of Motorcycling.

JERE'S ANTIQUES
9 Jefferson St, Savannah, 912-236-2815
www.jeresantiques.com
Since 1973, this shop has been a favorite of collectors, designers and auction houses. The owner maintains a warehouse in England with buyers working throughout Britain as well as in Belgium, Holland and France. Owner Jere Myers maintains his own warehouse in England and has buyers and pickers working throughout Britain and on the continent in Belgium, Holland and France. With a constant supply of new inventory, shoppers can discover a variety of treasures like an 18th century chest, a 19th century breakfront or an Art Deco vanity.

KELLER'S FLEA MARKET

5901 Ogeechee Rd, Savannah, 912-927-4848
www.ilovefleas.com
Popular among locals and tourists, this flea market
has over 400 retail stall spaces and six food
concessions. The flea market has showers for
traveling vendors, handicap access and a barbershop.
Here you'll find a variety of unique, unusual, and
even useful merchandise at bargain prices.

KOBO GALLERY

33 Barnard St, Savannah, 912-201-0304
www.kobogallery.com
Located adjacent to Ellis Square, this gallery features
a co-op atmosphere with a group of local artists that
include: Christi Reiterman, Daniel E. Smith, David J.
Kaminsky, and Dicky Stone.

LEOPOLD'S ICE CREAM

212 E Broughton St, Savannah, 912-234-4442
www.leopoldsicecream.com
This beautiful store was designed by Academy Award nominated designer Dan Lomino and it's filled with props, posters, and signed photographs of actors. The shop includes much of the original 1935 décor including the original soda fountain, back bar, sundae holders, and banana split boats. A local's favorites because of the original, secret ice cream recipes.

MADAME CHRYSANTHEMUM

101 W Taylor St, Savannah, 912-238-3355
https://madamechrysanthemum.com/
This beautiful shop offers a variety of flowers and gifts. You'll not only find amazing flowers but an assortment of things for the garden, candles, jewelry, stationary, and a few odds and ends for the house.

MALDOROR'S FRAME SHOP

2418 De Soto Ave, Savannah, 912-443-5355
No Website
A frame shop with the aura of a Victorian curio shop, featuring antique prints, custom framing and woodworking.

OGLETHORPE MALL

7804 Abercorn St, Savannah, 912-629-2800
www.oglethorpemall.com
Oglethorpe is a regional shopping mall with a food court, a carousel, and a variety of name stores including: Belk, JCPenney, Macy's, Sears, Old Navy, Hello Kitty, and Stein Mart.

ONE FISH TWO FISH

401 Whitaker St, 912-447-4600
www.onefishstore.com
This shop exudes "coastal cool" with its eclectic
inventory of trendy jewelry, LouenHide handbags,
Pine Cone Hill linens, Archipelago Botanical bath
and body products or Mariposa glossy pewter serving
and entertaining pieces. And you'll fall in love with
the cute honeybee embellishments on the straw or
fabric handbags by Bosom Buddy Bags.

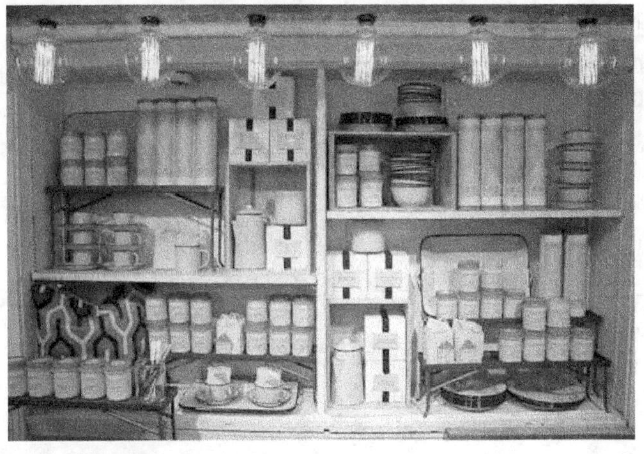

THE PARIS MARKET

36 W Broughton St., 912-232-1500
www.theparismarket.com
Owners Paula and Taras Danyluk travel the world and
fill their fascinating little shop with goods they think
you can't live without. You'll find Savons de
Marseille blocks of olive oil soap (I love these great
soaps) as well as small cotton bags of imported
lavender. Downstairs you'll find a sprinkling of

antiques and even vintage sacred items such as an old church altar, Madonna statue and Santa Rosa candles from Mexico. Here you'll find collections from Milan, Rome, Florence, England, as well as from the flea markets of Hungary, Holland, Belgium, and Paris. Here you'll find a world of treasures including everything from handbags, jewelry, architectural finds, teacups, perfume, and furniture. Local artists rotate their artwork through the shop.

PARKERS MARKET

222 Drayton St, Savannah, 912-233-1000
https://parkerskitchen.com/market/
Regional convenience store that combines a gas station with a Fresh Market.

PLANTATION JEWELS

502 E River St, Savannah, 912-667-4608
www.mkt.com/plantation-jewels WEBSITE DOWN AT PRESSTIME
This shop features the handcrafted jewelry made by owners Paul and Jeanie Chance. Every piece comes with a Story Book telling the history of the item. The artists use antique glass shards, antique china shards, and antique buttons that they have collected to make wearable art.

RIVER STREET MARKET PLACE

502 E River St, Savannah, 912-629-2647
https://riverstreetmarketplace.com/
Experience this unique open-air shopping market next to the river featuring more than 50 vendors. Vendors

offer a wide range of shopping including photography, art, and unusual imports.

SAINTS AND SHAMROCKS
309 Bull St, Savannah, 912-233-8858
www.saintsandshamrocks.com
Located in the heart of Downtown, this shop specializes in Irish imports and Catholic gifts. This shop services the needs of Savannah's Irish Catholic community.

104 W Broughton St, Savannah, 912-233-7873
www.savannahbee.com
Befitting its name, here you'll find a variety of pure
and naturally organic honey products and beauty
supplies. You'll find products such as honey and
comb, beeswax-centric bath and body products, mint
julep lip balm, and a variety of luxurious beeswax-
based body care products. There's even a honey
tasting station up front.

SAVANNAH CANDY KITCHEN-CITY MARKET

318 E Saint Julian Street, Savannah, 912-201-9501
www.savannahcandy.com
All lovers of sweets come to this place because it's
filled with homemade goodies like pralines or
gophers — pecan clusters covered with caramel and
chocolate.

SAVANNAH MALL

14045 Abercorn St, Savannah, 912-521-9670
www.savannahmall.com
Located on the south side of Savannah, this is an enclosed regional shopping mall with four anchor stores: Bass Pro Shops, Burlington Coat Factory, Dillard's and Target.

SEVENTH HEAVEN ANTIQUES
3104 Skidaway Rd., 912-355-0835
www.antiquesinsavannah.com
This low-slung building on Skidaway Road is easy to miss driving by, but you'll want to make a U-turn for this stellar shop loaded with early American furniture, china and jewelry. Its odds and ends range from a math book from 1878 to an Italian Palumba accordion, not to mention a variety of clocks, Canton blue china (circa 1850), colorful Majolica dishes (circa 1870).

SHOPSCAD
340 Bull St, Savannah, 912-525-5180
www.shopscad.com
Located in Poetter Hall, this shop is a showcase for
items designed and created by the students of
Savannah College of Art and Design. Here you'll find
treasures like jewelry, painting, baby blankets,
greeting cards, towels, sculpture, handbags, clothing,
photography and pottery.

V&J DUNCAN
12 East Taylor St, Savannah, 912-232-0338
www.vjduncan.com
Located in the Historic District, this shop offers a
unique variety of antique maps, prints and books.
Here you'll find a vast collection of old engravings,
mezzotints, lithographs, photographs, old books and
books from Savannah authors like autographed copies
of the classic "Midnight in the Garden of Good and
Evil."

INDEX

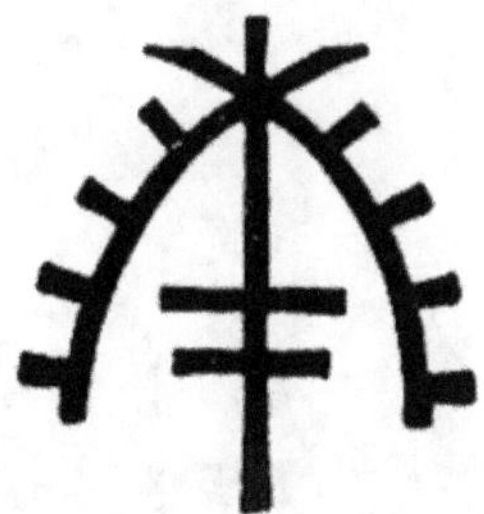